If I were to describe New Orlea[ns] exquisitely beautiful but slightly experienced in the ways of the v[orld] come-hither decadence, who is not to be underestimated. There's a sense of the exotic about her; and an ever-present threat – or promise – of trickery permeates her French Quarter's narrow streets and shuttered Creole cottages. It dances down Frenchmen Street to the brassy beat of street musicians, pan handlers and yard spinners, all with smiles as bright as the sun.

A decade after the storm to end all storms, the city has morphed into something else entirely. It has survived and thrived. Living here, I feel as though adventure has happened all around me, and will still happen again and again. I love it.

the hunt new orleans writer

beth d'addono

Beth D'Addono is a food and travel writer who fell head over heels in love with New Orleans more than 20 years ago. Unable to resist the city's magnetic allure, Beth moved from Philadelphia to the Marigny in 2012. A passionate supporter of the city's vibrant food, music and arts culture, she spends her non-working hours riding her bike, listening to live music, walking her dog Ruby along the river and connecting with the particular New Orleans brand of magical realism that greets her every time she walks out of her front door. Nothing makes her happier than discovering and sharing all things Nola beyond the limited and overrated Bourbon Street, and working on assembling a respectable costume closet.

BON MAISON GUEST HOUSE

where to lay
your weary head

Rest up, relax and recharge

1896 O'MALLEY HOUSE

Elegance with a Mid-City address

120 South Pierce Street (between Cleveland and Canal) / +1 504 488 5896

1896omalleyhouse.com

Standard double from $155

When I travel, I love to stay in well-located neighborhoods away from the tourist fray. If you're the same, head to Mid-City's elegant 1896 O'Malley House, a Bed & Breakfast with a charming courtyard and convenient location close to bunches of Carrollton Avenue eats and services. The location off the Canal Streetcar line is a 15-minute ride from the French Quarter. The owners and hosts, Brad and Larry, earn high marks for being helpful but never intrusive.

AUDUBON COTTAGES

Luxurious romantic retreat in the Quarter

509 Dauphine Street (between Toulouse and Saint Louis) / +1 504 586 1516
auduboncottages.com

Standard rates from $399

Imagine having a rich friend who is in the South of France for her annual sojourn and was generous enough to leave you the key to her secluded French Quarter hideaway. That's what it feels like to stay in one of the seven refurbished Audubon Cottages, named for former resident John James Audubon. If it's high end, über private and spacious intimate digs you crave, crave no more. I love the saltwater pool in the courtyard and, of course, the in-room spa services are divine. It'll cost you, but what a treat.

B&W COURTYARDS

You'll never want to leave this Marigny hideaway

2425 Chartres Street (between Spain and Mandeville) / +1 504 322 0474
bandwcourtyards.com

Standard double from $159

It may be just a few blocks from where I live, but I yearn for a staycation at
B&W Courtyards in the Marigny. Owners Tom and Dana are only the fourth to care
for this Creole gem that dates back to 1854, and their stewardship is clearly a
labor of love. The courtyard is a blissful garden complete with a pond and each
room has been painstakingly restored with antiques and upscale amenities.
You're close to restaurants and not far from Frenchmen Street, without
the hubbub. Simply put, B&W is like staying with friends.

AUDUBON COTTAGES

BON MAISON GUEST HOUSE

A haven on the residential end of Bourbon

835 Bourbon Street (between Dumain and Saint Ann) / +1 504 561 8498
bonmaison.com

Standard double from $140

Bon Maison Guest House is a perfect fit if you want to be near the action, but not in the middle of it. Situated on the more residential end of Bourbon Street, this quaint 1833 town house is an ideal home base. Nothing fancy here, but prices are good, the rooms are well appointed and comfortable, the patio is lush and verdant and you're just a block from one of my favorite bars, Lafitte's.

THE LOOKOUT INN

Locally owned inn with cool Bywater vibe

833 Poland Avenue (between Burgundy and Dauphine) / +1 504 947 8188
lookoutneworleans.com

Standard double from $99

If you need to walk out your front door into the French Quarter, The Lookout Inn isn't for you. But if you're like me, and adore a pet-friendly stay in a real neighborhood, then step right up. Decorated with an eye to color and comfort with themes like Mardi Gras and Elvis, the suites offer roomy baths and boatloads of panache. You're close to eateries favored by locals, and can walk to bars and restaurants on artsy Saint Claude (see pg 32).

THE LOOKOUT INN

bywater

When I first became addicted to New Orleans in the early '90s, the Bywater neighborhood in the Upper Ninth Ward seemed like the hinterlands, even though it wasn't that far from the Marigny, where I used to stay while visiting and where I now live. I'd venture to see jazz legend Kermit Ruffins at his then-regular Thursday night gigs at Vaughan's Lounge and worry about a cab showing up to take me home. Now, this ramshackle 'hood that follows the river to the Industrial Canal is buzzing. Architecturally intriguing, it's a residential haven of small, locally owned restaurants and businesses that thrum with the vitality of this city. In recent years, real estate prices have sky-rocketed and locals worry, with good reason, about the area losing its Nola-specific cache. That hasn't happened yet, but don't dawdle. Explore now.

1 Bacchanal
2 Bon Castor
3 Booty's Street Food
4 Euclid Records
5 Frady's One Stop Food Store
6 Red's Chinese
7 Satsuma Café
8 Sugar Park

11

BACCHANAL

Wine bar and outdoor restaurant with live music

600 Poland Avenue (corner of Chartres) / +1 504 948 9111
bacchanalwine.com / Open daily

Bacchanal is the kind of place where Quentin Tarantino can show up to watch Seville-worthy flamenco in the spacious courtyard, and no one bats an eye. This hybrid hangout attracts artists, foodies and locals to chill, graze and listen to live music on the edge of the Bywater. The vibe is nonchalant, both in the charming courtyard, where you can nibble on cheese and charcuterie platters, and in the gastropub upstairs where you can tuck into more substantial eats. Also, of course, befitting its name, Bacchanal serves a decadent selection of wines by the glass or bottle. There's a vino store up front if you need to stock up on the way home.

BON CASTOR

All New Orleans-made wares

3207 Burgundy Street (at Louisa) / +1 504 948 9987
boncastor.com / Closed Monday

When I want to treat myself, I go to Bon Castor, Amy Knoll's funky boutique
selling locally made goods. The shop's name, which means "by hand,"
is a clue that it showcases crafts, repurposed textiles and fashion, gifts
and jewelry, all made by the local hands of some 80 artists. You'll also find
hand-sewn baby bibs and vinyl records turned into whimsical clocks by
Bayou Saint John artist Judy Gamache DiGeorge. My last purchase was
a sassy purple dress from Esther Rose; an asymmetrical mini with
unhemmed edges, bits of tulle and sequin fringe, a fab frock straight
out of *A Midsummer Night's Dream* if it was set in the future. Be warned
though, you'll have to try on clothes as there are no size labels on the
garments sold here.

BOOTY'S STREET FOOD

International noshing

800 Louisa Street (at Dauphine) / +1 504 266 2887
bootysnola.com / Open daily

Booty's globetrotting owners Nick and Kevin couldn't find a
neighborhood bar that satisfied their worldly tastes in eats and
craft cocktails. So they opened one, with a menu mined from their
travels in Mexico, Malaysia, Singapore and Israel. Settle in to the
compact space, and choose from the likes of grilled octopus served with
gochujang (a Korean chili and fermented soybean paste), or Vietnamese
pork belly bánh mì. The inventive cocktail list credits each drink's creator,
so thank you Jenny Cobb for Sweater Weather, made with fig-infused
vodka, sage, honey and lemon. Plates are made for sharing, but you may
not feel like it once you take your first bite.

EUCLID RECORDS

Vinyl emporium

3301 Chartres Street (at Piety) / +1 504 947 4348 / euclidnola.com
Open daily

It doesn't get more personal than Euclid Records. This haven for
all things vinyl represents the passionate vision of a trio of buds;
New Orleans transplants with ties to Saint Louis and New York. The store
is an outgrowth of the Saint Louis Euclid Records, but is New Orleans
through and through. It's the kind of place you can hang and browse until
you find that vintage copy of Al Green's Greatest Hits. About 15 percent of
the store's stock supports New Orleans artists; the rest is an eclectic array
of roughly 70,000 pieces of music, most of which is vinyl. Simply put,
if you're a lover of vinyl, Euclid is the record store of your dreams.

FRADY'S ONE STOP FOOD STORE

He-Man portions at a local gem

3231 Dauphine Street (at Piety) / +1 504 949 9688
facebook.com/pages/Fradys-One-Stop-Food-Store / Closed Sunday

Frady's One Stop Food Store dishes up hot, homemade food at rock
bottom prices, and always with a smile. The family-owned neighborhood
shop doesn't look like much from the outside, but follow the long line of
cabbies, cops and carpenters inside and you'll find groceries and plate
lunches that might include fried chicken or liver and onions, and red beans
and rice, priced around $7. And did I mention it serves some of the best
damn sandwiches on the planet? Get the roast beef po-boy, and be sure to
ask for extra napkins. Just don't expect to pull out the plastic when it comes
to paying. As the low prices might suggest, it's a cash-only joint.

RED'S CHINESE

Feisty fusion of Creole and Sichuan

3048 Saint Claude Avenue (at Clouet) / +1 504 304 6030
redschinese.com / Closed Tuesday

This city has an Achilles heel when it comes to restaurants: real
Chinese food, especially mouth-searing Sichuan cuisine. That's changing
though, and thanks in part to Red's Chinese. Chef and co-owner
Tobias Womack and partner Amy Mosberger learned to riff off of
traditional recipes from James Beard award-winning chef Danny Bowien
of Mission Chinese Food fame. The duo adds Creole touches and local
ingredients to dishes like kung pao pastrami, a Mission Chinese staple,
in this case made with Louisiana's holy trinity of onions, bell peppers
and celery. Bold flavors of garlic, chili and ginger inform a menu that is
as unorthodox as it is habit-forming. You might need a stretcher after an
order of fiery smoked mushrooms and tofu, but you'll go out grinning.

SATSUMA CAFÉ

Healthy food choices in a cool neighborhood

3218 Dauphine Street (between Louisa and Piety) / +1 504 304 5962
satsumacafe.com / Open daily

New Orleans isn't a place known for gastronomic restraint.
Indulging occasionally on cream sauces and fried seafood is one thing,
making it a lifestyle is quite another. That's why Satsuma Café is such
a delight. Freshly squeezed veggie and fruit juices, like the kale and
spinach-powered Popeye, and substantial salads made with seasonal
local produce are just the ticket to avoid becoming Fat City. I can still
order decadent French toast with caramelized apples or an oozy cheese
and bacon sandwich if the mood strikes, or stick with a vegan tofu
scramble and call it good. It's nice to have options, all served in a space
that's pure come-as-you-are casual.

SUGAR PARK

Divine pizza in a living room setting

3054 Saint Claude Avenue (at Clouet) / +1 504 942 2047
sugarparknola.com / Closed Mondays

This eclectic eatery is still relatively undiscovered. That may change when the streetcar expands down Saint Claude in 2016, but in the meantime expect to rub elbows with locals convening over pizza and tasty grub from burgers to fresh salads and the fried goodness of Yum-Yums — artichoke and mozzarella served with marinara sauce. Pizza chef and co-owner Stephen Polier is a former New Yorker, and his pies definitely have an accent. I love the quirky A Pizza Named Desire, a toothsome crust slathered with crawfish, sausage and jalapeño. The service is friendly, drinks strong and cheap, and the portions are generous. What's not to like?

faubourg marigny

A few blocks from the honky-tonk of Bourbon Street, just up from where the Mississippi bends into its famous crescent, is the place I call home. Bordering the French Quarter to the north is Faubourg Marigny, an original Creole neighborhood named after 19th-century aristocrat and good-time-guy Bernard de Marigny de Mandeville. In 1800, when his father died, Marigny became the richest 15-year-old in America, inheriting a vast fortune and the plantation that once defined the neighborhood. In typical Big Easy style, Marigny gambled away the family homestead (he's credited with creating the game of craps), but his loss was the city's gain, because in my book, the Marigny, with its Creole cottages, nighttime art market, indie shops and eclectic restaurants, is the sweetest place in town.

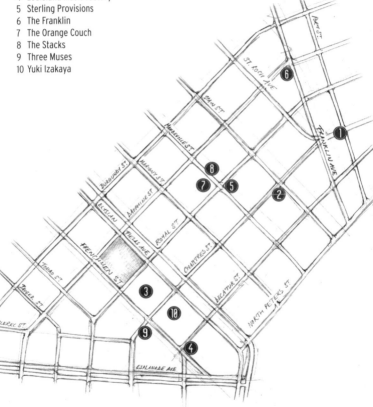

BAO AND NOODLE

Authentic Chinese

2700 Chartres Street (at Port) / +1 504 272 0004
baoandnoodle.com / Closed Sunday and Monday

I almost burst into tears when I tasted Chef Doug Crowell's divine fried and steamed bao stuffed with soy flavored garlicky roast pork. A veteran of the Herbsaint kitchen, Crowell is married to a Chinese-American, whose father is a New York chef. Every time he visited his in-laws, the table groaned with homemade Chinese food, and Crowell paid attention. Prices are reasonable at this BYO, whether you're sharing a steamed whole local fish stuffed with lemongrass or a plate of zippy dandan noodles. The ma po tofu isn't quite spicy enough for me, and I'd love to see more veggie options, but I'm not complaining. What I am is a regular.

CAKE CAFÉ AND BAKERY

Down-home baking

2440 Chartres Street (at Spain) / +1 504 943 0010
nolacakes.com / Closed Tuesday

Cake Café had me at goat cheese and apple king cake — exactly the kind of beyond the usual deliciousness that makes this place rock. No mere bakery this, although the pastries are divine and the cupcakes only cost a buck with any order. Instead, Steve Himlefarb's gem is homespun heaven, a no frills neighborhood breakfast and lunch joint that dishes shrimp and grits, boudin and eggs and crawfish omelets. In a city tough on vegetarians, the sesame-crusted fried tofu sandwich with pesto, roasted tomatoes and cucumber is a revelation. And that apple and goat cheese king cake I mentioned? That alone makes Mardi Gras both sweet and savory.

FRENCHMEN ART MARKET

Al fresco art and treasures

619 Frenchmen Street (between Chartres and Royal)
+1 504 941 1149 / facebook.com/Frenchmenartmarket / Open evening,
Thursday to Sunday

A beehive of locally made art and jewelry, this brightly lit night market boasts a revolving roster of quirky artists creating everything from whimsical flatware sculptures to Impressionist style streetcar scenes and inventive T-shirt designs. Right in the heart of Frenchmen Street nuttiness, this is where locals in the know buy their gifts and art for wall and wearing. Check out the fun feathered hair barrettes or pick up a circus sideshow scene painted on wood by a pretty young woman with facial tattoos. I always leave time to head to the uplit couch in the back, to sit a spell and people watch.

LOUISIANA MUSIC FACTORY

A treasure trove of Nola tunes

421 Frenchmen Street (at Decatur) / +1 504 586 1094
louisianamusicfactory.com / Open daily

The best place in the neighborhood to buy music (and let's face it, you can't download vinyl) is Louisiana Music Factory, located in airy digs in the heart of the action on Frenchmen Street. This spacious store is staffed by helpful nerds well-read on both local releases and the national jazz scene. There's a decent selection of records too, and a big bonus: an ongoing schedule of free concerts showcasing some of the top talent in town. It's not unusual to see a popular local musician like Craig Klein from Bonerama show up, with his battered trombone case in hand.

STERLING PROVISIONS

Mid-century furnishings and home accessories

2402 Royal Street (at Mandeville) / +1 917 309 0259
sterlingprov.com / Closed Monday

Quirky and cool, this vintage furniture and homeware boutique is a
perfect fit for the Marigny. Whether it's mid-century, Danish modern
or retro kitsch you have in mind, there's something here to fit the bill.
I long for the Bernhardt cut velvet pillows, or maybe I really want the
faux fur sham? Howard's brand wood oils are on the shelf too, along
with handmade small batch soaps and soy candles. The lot of it is
curated by New York City transplant Dennis Weddle, who has a keen eye
for offbeat serving pieces, lamps and furnishings with natural elements
of wood, ceramic and plaster.

THE FRANKLIN

Urban elegance for dinner

2600 Dauphine Street (at Franklin) / +1 504 267 0640
thefranklinnola.com / Open evening daily

The Franklin is guaranteed to impress your baby on date night.
This restaurant exchanges the usual quirky downtown vibe for an
elegant setting worthy of Chef Zack Tippen's refined French-inspired
seasonal cuisine. Most of the small plates are intriguing, especially
slices of tender rare filet served à la mode with foie gras ice cream.
Try grilled oysters with garlic butter or fried with a luscious white
rémoulade on the side, or tuck into smoky shrimp and grits with bacon
or a perfect coq au vin. Add a spectacular wine and cocktail list, and this
downtown restaurant becomes very uptown indeed.

THE ORANGE COUCH

A modern neighborhood café

2339 Royal Street (corner of Mandeville) / +1 504 267 7327
facebook.com/page/Orange-Couch / Open daily

When I need to schedule a meeting that deserves a little more elbow room than my apartment can offer, I go to The Orange Couch, which has outdoor seating so my dog Ruby can sometimes come along too. The sleek meeting spot is full of 20- and 30-somethings on their laptops, drinking excellent lattes. It's the kind of place where you're as likely to strike up a conversation with a suited politico as you are with a girl in neon tights producing a documentary for the BBC. The *New York Times* is available at the counter, and they serve a swell line of Japanese ice cream and buzz-worthy Vietnamese iced coffee ideal for a sweltering day.

THE STACKS

Modish haven of art books

2402 Royal Street (at Mandeville) / +1 504 439 0846
thestacks-books.org / Closed Monday

If I want to buy a special gift for an artsy friend, I often turn to this little
indie bookstore. The realized vision of owner Émilie Lamy, a lovely French
artist with a spot-on sense of style and merchandising, The Stacks is a
permanent pop up in the middle of the extremely cool Sterling Provisions.
Émilie artfully displays tomes focused on visual and graphic arts,
architecture, photography, music, new media, and creative source material.
Choose from an eclectic and sassy selection of contemporary art books,
from exhibition catalogs to monographs, theory publications, as well as
a wide range of international magazines. A changing selection of local art
is also on display, to add to your browsing pleasure.

THREE MUSES

A siren song of refined libations, food and music

536 Frenchmen Street (between Chartres and Decatur)
+1 504 252 4801 / 3musesnola.com / Closed Tuesday

I'm a small plates fiend. Appetizers are always my favorite part of a meal, so the tapas at Three Muses are always a hit. The nicely balanced menu is literally all over the map, with the likes of a deviled yard egg with crackling featured alongside a delectable cheese plate. You can also order stuffed shells, Korean rice bowls or crawfish tamale. My friend Sammye swoons over the Two Run Farms lamb sliders slathered with goat cheese, but I almost always order the irresistible seared scallops with smoky sweet bacon. Also an intimate and eclectic music venue, this small place often commands a line, even with reservations. Good thing the cocktails are top shelf.

YUKI IZAKAYA

Funky Japanese bar and tasty nibbles

525 Frenchmen Street (between Decatur and Chartres)
+1 504 943 1122 / facebook.com/yukiizakaya / Open daily

My Japanese sister-in-law has a delicate constitution. While my brother and I can slam back anything from dirty martinis and fried chicken to a full on tasting menu, this poor lamb is all sixes and sevens unless she gets her ramen. Thank goodness for Yuki Izakaya on Frenchmen Street, just a few blocks from my place. It may look like a divey hole in the wall, but this dimly lit tavern has a respectable sake list along with authentic Japanese treats like tasty ramen, octopus dumplings and spicy cod roe pickles. The entertainment is eclectic too — on any given night, you might hear French Algerian Norbert Slama play accordion or see vintage Japanese gangster movies play on a brick backdrop.

ALLWAYS LOUNGE & THEATRE
2240 Saint Claude Avenue (at Marigny), +1 504 218 5778
theallwayslounge.net, open daily

ARABELLA CASA DI PASTA
2258 Saint Claude Avenue (between Marigny and
Mandeville), +1 504 267 6108, arabellanola.com
closed Sunday

JUNCTION
3021 Saint Claude Avenue (between Montegut and
Feliciana), +1 504 272 0205, junctionNOLA.com
open daily

KAJUN'S PUB
2256 Saint Claude Avenue (between Mandeville and
Spain), +1 504 947 3735, kajunpub.com, open daily

KEBAB
2315 Saint Claude Avenue (between Mandeville
and Spain), +1 504 383 4328, kebabnola.com
closed Tuesday to Thursday

OLD MARQUER THEATRE
2400 Saint Claude Avenue (at Saint Roch)
+1 504 298 8676, oldmarquer.com
closed Monday and Tuesday

SATURN BAR
3067 Saint Claude Avenue (at Clouet), +1 504 949 7532
saturnbar.com, open daily

SIBERIA
2227 Saint Claude Avenue (between Elysian Fields
and Marigny), +1 504 265 8855, siberianola.com
open daily

Savoring the avenue

Those of a certain mindset in search of a fresh vibe and an alternative to crowded Frenchmen Street have the artsy Saint Claude Corridor in their sights. Rooted in the city's post-Katrina hurricane influx of artists and new residents, this gritty stretch along the "New Marigny" and Bywater includes a growing number of pubs, theaters and restaurants joining longstanding venues like **Saturn Bar** to create nuevo New Orleans late night destinations.

For dinner, I already told you about **Red's Chinese** (pg 17) and **Sugar Park** (pg 19) in Bywater. Then there's **Arabella Casa di Pasta**, a build-your-own pasta emporium with house-made noodles and a handful of better-than-mama's sauces. **Kebab**, a Middle Eastern storefront eatery, has grilled marinated meats piled onto crusty rolls baked in house and dressed with tzatziki, aioli, or their special garlicky herbaceous sauce called skhug. **Junction** is all about local and craft beer, and satisfying bar food including burgers, fries and wings.

For music and a show, the **AllWays Lounge & Theatre** is a great little avant-garde bar spotlighting performance art and burlesque. You can take a swing dance lesson most Sundays and drag shows are often an option. **Siberia** is hard to categorize, a live rock/Goth/heavy metal/Balkans folk/comedy venue, nice and dark, with a pool table, creepy taxidermy and beat up tables and chairs. The newly renamed **Old Marquer Theatre**, formerly The Shadowbox, is a drug store turned theater which stages burlesque, drama and comedy shows five nights a week. Best known for its rockin' karaoke, the sprightly horseshoe shaped bar of **Kajun's Pub** is also a great place to hang during a game or the random spoken word performance on a Sunday afternoon.

the french quarter

Jackson Square to Esplanade

Head down river toward Esplanade from the 700 block of streets like Royal, Chartres, Bourbon and Dauphine, and things quiet down a bit in the French Quarter. There's a cluster of gay bars on this section of Bourbon, along with the supposedly haunted pub Lafitte's; there's also a postal emporium, a frame shop, and always the pleasure of lush courtyards glimpsed through lacy wrought iron gates. Armstrong Park on Rampart is a refreshing bit of green space filled with music-themed art. Decatur is more commercial, home to tourists and pan handlers, and a quirky mix of shops and eateries, as well as the busy French Market. But really everywhere you stroll, the lovely architecture and burnished beauty of this neighborhood captivates.

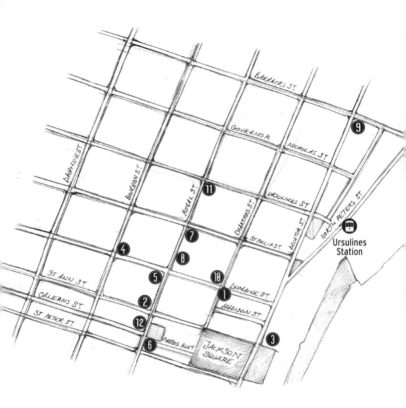

1 Animal Art Antiques
2 Bourbon French Parfums
3 Café du Monde
4 Clover Grill
5 Craig Tracy's Fine-Art Bodypainting Gallery
6 Faulkner House Books

7 Fifi Mahony's
8 La Madama Bazarre
9 Le Garage Antiques & Clothing
10 Moonshine Nettie
11 Nadine Blake
12 Trashy Diva Lingerie

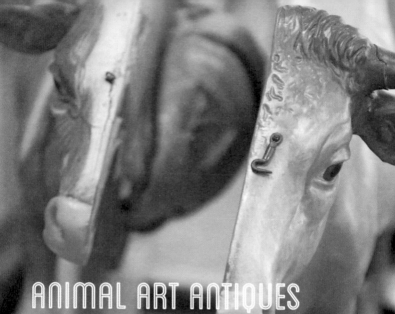

ANIMAL ART ANTIQUES

Creatures as art, from majestic to macabre

824 Chartres Street (between Dumaine and Saint Ann)
+1 504 525 8005 / animalartantiques.com
Closed Monday and Tuesday, or by appointment

Inside Animal Art Antiques, eyes seem to follow you everywhere, some of them from critters long stuffed for posterity. But mostly this interesting shop offers truly spectacular animal-themed antiques, like the beady-eyed 19th-century French Majolica rooster I've been hankering after; or the brass floor lamp with custom-made pheasant-feather shades snagged from a French flea market. There are gorgeous botanical drawings and a French engraving of a monkey from Diderot's *Histoire Naturelle* that is particularly winsome. Most items are simply pretty, and the owners are graceful and calming, even if those Victorian-era mechanical bulldogs look like they might rip you to shreds.

BOURBON FRENCH PARFUMS

Olfactory history and seduction

805 Royal Street (between Dumaine and Saint Ann)
+1 504 522 4480 / neworleansperfume.com / Open daily

Where have the real parfumeries gone? Part art, part alchemy, these were places where trained professionals matched you with a bespoke scent or a customized aroma based on your personality, tastes and own particular eau de sweat. Thank heaven for Bourbon French Parfums, where fragrances are still blended the old fashioned way. The shop's back room acts as a mixology laboratory, while the large display up front holds elegant cut-glass bottles and blends such as the signature Kus Kus scent, dating back to when the shop opened in the 1840s. My fave is Voodoo Love, an ode to storied queen Marie Laveau; think love potion number nine, turned up to 11.

CAFÉ DU MONDE

Beignets from heaven

800 Decatur Street (corner of Saint Ann) / +1 504 525 4544
cafedumonde.com / Open daily

While walking my dog Ruby along the river from Esplanade to
the Aquarium, one of my favorite early morning New Orleans sights is
tourists sitting on benches across from Café du Monde eating beignets,
clouds of powdered sugar swirling in the air like gnats on an August eve.
These deep-fried pillows of dough, served 24/7 at the open air café, come
three to an order, and are best enjoyed with chicory-laced café au lait on
the side. (Note to self – payment is cash only). There's a shop across the
street that sells Café du Monde coffee along with beignet mix, but I warn
you, the real deal version of this doughnut is tough to replicate at home.

CLOVER GRILL

Quintessential diner – the disco version

900 Bourbon Street (corner of Dumaine) / +1 504 598 1010
clovergrill.com / Open daily

Open every hour of every day, the Clover Grill's motto is "We love to
fry and it shows." It is known for its juicy (and cheap!) burgers, cooked
under a trademark hub cap, but this is more than a greasy spoon.
It's also a floor show in one of the most colorful, diverse, let-your-freak-
flag-fly neighborhoods in the city. It's an experience late at night, what
with the gay bars and the honky-tonks of Bourbon just up the street.
Pretty boys in hot pants groove to the Zapp Band while taking your
order and the grill masters are maestros, effortlessly manning dozens of
pans at once. It makes for quite the spectacle, I assure you.

CRAIG TRACY'S FINE-ART BODYPAINTING GALLERY

The human form as a canvas

827 Royal Street (between Dumaine and Saint Ann)
+1 504 592 9886 / craigtracy.com / Open daily

You won't believe your eyes when you step inside Craig Tracy's Fine-Art
Bodypainting Gallery. The artist creates at the intersection of fine art
and body painting, transforming bodies of all shapes and sizes into
air-brushed masterpieces. From surreal to realistic landscapes to nature
to ethnic to out of this world, Tracy decides what to paint depending on
the shape of the particular body. He then photographs the subject in an art
directed setting, sometimes against another backdrop, sometimes focused
on the form itself. The result is startlingly original and certainly not like
anything else you'll see in any of the other galleries along Royal Street.

FAULKNER HOUSE BOOKS

Southern-focused lit in Faulkner's old digs

624 Pirates Alley (between Chartres and Royal) / +1 504 524 2940
faulknerhousebooks.com / Open daily

William Faulkner lived and wrote his first novel on these very premises in the 1920s. The author would no doubt approve of Faulkner House Books, the epitome of an old fashioned bookseller that occupies the downstairs space. The manager, Miss Joanne, is whip smart and a fount of knowledge about rare books regarding the South, with an emphasis on New Orleans- and Louisiana-related titles. Sifting through the dusty classics and finding a signed first edition has been known to happen here. Beware though: these shelves are so well curated that you come in looking for one book and might leave with 20.

FIFI MAHONY'S

Outrageous hair pieces and accessories

934 Royal Street (between Dumaine and Saint Philip)
+1 504 525 4343 / fifimahonys.com / Closed Saturday

Wigs are so liberating. I didn't know just how fab I'd feel in a cobalt pageboy until I discovered Fifi Mahony's on Royal Street. Home to towering pepto-pink bouffant wigs, glittery false eyelashes and bright peacock-sized feather headdresses, this place is a trip. Glamour pusses clamor for the outrageous theatrical makeup, spectacular wigs and accessories geared to show-stopping performances, drag or otherwise. Pay $5 for a stretchy hair cover – it goes towards your purchase – and you can try on options to see what looks great. Since you only live once, you might as well be fabulous every day and wear Fifi's to the supermarket. That's quite normal here because in New Orleans, what elsewhere might be considered outrageous is as common as Mardi Gras beads on Saint Charles Avenue.

LA MADAMA BAZARRE

Local art and oddities

910 Royal Street (between Saint Philip and Dumaine)
+1 504 236 5076 / lamadamabazarre.com / Closed Tuesday

The painting by Jason London Hawkins captivated me, a quartet of fallen Storyville beauties in red, smiling brazenly over feather fans. I especially loved that the local artist had painted across the borders of the antique frame that embraced the scene. Now on my bedroom wall, this was the beginning of my love affair with La Madama Bazarre, Jennifer Kirtlan's edgy, oh-so-non-traditional gallery. Much of what's on the walls here reminds me of the TV show *American Horror Story*, i.e. disturbing but impossible not to watch. The gallery, done up in surreal hot pink, dips freely into outsider art and nightmarish tableaus, all of which adds up to a wonderfully bizarre bazaar.

LE GARAGE
ANTIQUES & CLOTHING

Vintage and costume in the Quarter

1234 Decatur Street (at Barracks) / +1 504 522 6639
facebook.com/LeGarageNewOrleans / Closed Monday

It's fun to browse in this ramshackle labyrinth of odds and ends, and despite what seems to be a real sense of randomness to what's in store, the super-helpful staff will point you in the right direction. Your costuming options are both literally and metaphorically all over the shop – think military uniforms and swords; antebellum hoop skirts, sequined mermaid dresses, and leather chaps. Prices are reasonable and there's never any pressure to buy. When the boyfriend was an angel to go with my devil one year, we found the perfect white choir robe here as well as the feathered wings for a heavenly touch.

MOONSHINE NETTIE

Glitter punk and rock 'n' roll

901 Chartres Street (at Dumaine) / +1 504 544 5482
No website / Closed Sunday

When Ragin' Daisy pulled up stakes from town, I was bereft. Where else could I find irreverent gifts, hand-crafted accessories with attitude and country and western vintage? The sisters who ran it tried to leave, but they soon realized the error of their ways, and now they're back with Moonshine Nettie. Inspired by their mom and grandma, both named Nettie, this shop is all about sass and sensibility, not to mention a particular unabashed deep Southern style that celebrates eccentricity, juke joints, red lipstick, cowboy boots and anything carnival. This is the spot for unrestrained bling, over-the-top headdresses and vintage wedding gowns. So glad the girls are back.

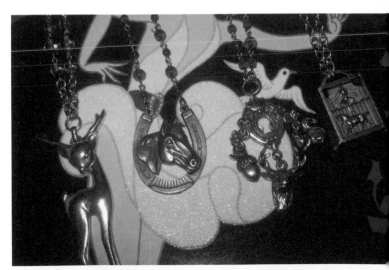

NADINE BLAKE

Smart Southern chic

1036 Royal Street (at Ursulines)   +1 504 529 4913
nadineblake.com   Closed Tuesday and Wednesday

There's more to tapping New Orleans style than looking for treasures in dusty antique shops. One-of-a-kind shop Nadine Blake combines regal antiques, vintage '60s Miami Beach, and talented local artisans' wares alongside modern European designs. The eponymously named store honors history but is committed to forward-thinking Southern style. Need a posh touch for a tired room? Try a patchwork pillow made from antique Indian textiles or natural soy wax candles in repurposed wine bottles. Nadine herself is a treasure, a friendly design maven happy to weigh in on paint color or textile choices — she'll even come to your castle and transform it, for a fee of course.

TRASHY DIVA LINGERIE

Retro naughty duds

712 Royal Street (between Saint Ann and Orleans)
+1 504 522 5686 / trashydiva.com / Open daily

If you think 1950s glamour puss Bettie Page is hot, you need to run, not walk, to Trashy Diva Lingerie. The boutique carries the kind of bad girlie lingerie guaranteed to quicken pulses. Yes, they have hard-to-find sizes and unmentionables for the curviest figure. They also stock *Mad Men*-era girdles and peignoirs. The brand had its start selling vintage 1940s and '50s fashion, with owner Candice Gwinn adding her own line of reimagined retro classics, outfits you won't see at the local mall, that's for sure. The shop also sells goodies like Victorian underbust corsets online, in case the irreverent beauty of your dreams is farther afield than Orleans Parish.

mardi gras magic

Beyond the super krewes

Contrary to popular thought, Mardi Gras isn't one day. This party starts on Twelfth Night and it goes on all the way to Fat Tuesday, as per the Advent calendar. The dates change from year to year though; mardigrasguide.com is a good place to check what's on, when.

Forget the drunken, flashing revelry on Bourbon Street – that's for tourists who don't know any better. The real Mardi Gras is a family affair marked by festive parades organized by krewes, the social clubs that work all year on themes, floats and costumes. Besides the trinity of super-krewes Rex, Endymion and Bacchus, there are smaller, quirkier parades that are must-sees for their authentic New Orleans verve.

The season kicks off with the always irreverent **Krewe du Vieux**, a satirical march through the Marigny of decorated, hand- or mule-drawn floats dripping with double entendre or in-your-face sassiness.

For sheer underdog charm, I adore **'tit Rex**, with its artsy types who fashion shoebox-sized mini-floats and hand pull them through the Saint Roch

KREWE DU VIEUX
Royal Street (at Franklin Avenue) to O'Keefe
kreweduvieux.org

KREWE OF BARKUS
Begins and ends in Armstrong Park
barkus.org

KREWE OF CHEWBACCHUS
Begins and ends in Saint Claude Avenue
chewbacchus.org

SOCIETÉ DE SAINT ANNE
Begins at Burgundy Street (at Piety)
kreweofsaintanne.org

'TIT REX
Saint Roch (at North Robertson) to Saint Claude
titrexparade.com

neighborhood into the Marigny. The name comes from the Cajun abbreviation of petite, commonly used as a prefix to the name of the younger of two people.

No dog lover can resist **Krewe of Barkus**, a parade of four-legged critters dressed to the nines, stealing the show from their human escorts.

The intergalactic **Krewe of Chewbacchus** is a sci-fi themed parade that steps off in the Ninth Ward and travels through the Marigny. Even though I'm not a fan of the genre, I love the self-propelled float contraptions built onto bicycles, homemade trailers and shopping carts.

But my all time favorite is the brilliantly costumed march of **Societé de Saint Anne**, an array of nutty creatives who parade from Bywater into the French Quarter, stopping at bars to celebrate along the way.

the french quarter

Canal to Jackson Square

This part of the French Quarter is the hub of tourism in New Orleans, an area prized for its Old World spirit, infinitely varied architecture and faded elegance. I love to walk my dog Ruby around the edges: along the river, up Canal, across Rampart and down leafy Esplanade – around the neighborhood where people live, not just where tourists visit. On the up-river side of the Quarter, between Canal Street and the 700 block of streets that flow along the Mississippi, a mix of French and Spanish architecture, Creole townhouses, boutiques, restaurants and hotels keep good company. Street buskers are everywhere, and Bourbon Street is at its most raucous in this part of town, with bars and souvenir shops bracketed by strip clubs and juke joints.

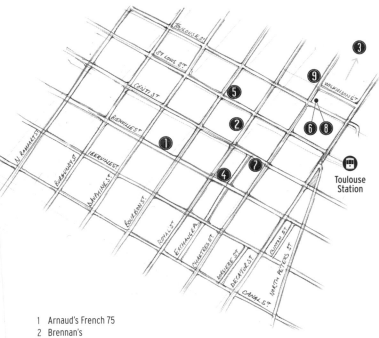

1 Arnaud's French 75
2 Brennan's
3 French Quarter Gem & Lapidary (off map)
4 Green Goddess
5 Kitchen Witch
6 Lucullus
7 NOLA Kids
8 Quarter Past Time
9 Sylvain

ARNAUD'S FRENCH 75

A grande dame

813 Bienville Street (between Bourbon and Dauphine)
+1 504 523 5433 / arnaudsrestaurant.com/french-75 / Open daily

Barman Chris Hannah has a statue of himself behind the bar, made by a fan – just one sign that his drinks inspire adoration. Arnaud's French 75 is the place to come if you want to sample an authentic New Orleans Sazerac or the namesake French 75, made with Cognac not gin.
The classic New Orleans eatery has been drawing a well heeled crowd since the 1920s to munch on soufflé, potatoes and oysters. Photographs of famous visitors line the staircase in the back, which leads up to a slightly eerie but utterly fantastic Mardi Gras museum. Take note of the bar, custom-built in the late 1800s for a restaurant on the Gulf Coast

BRENNAN'S

A legend makes a comeback

**417 Royal Street (between Saint Louis and Conti) / +1 504 525 9711
brennansneworleans.com / Closed Monday (January to March)**

Reopened in late 2014 after a $20 million renovation, locals are thrilled to have the storied Brennan's back, complete with the frenzied Breakfast at Brennan's tradition. The restaurant has anchored Creole dining on Royal Street since 1946, and now, with restaurateur Ralph Brennan and his partner Terry White at the helm, it's even more stunning. I love the bar, with its aviary theme and silvered mirror painted with peacocks and flamingos. Peachy pink accents the dining spaces, and a lavish private dining space upstairs celebrates the colors of Mardi Gras. Chef Slade Rushing reimagines Brennan's classics like Eggs Sardou and turtle soup while bringing his own Southern-influenced French cuisine and locally sourced dishes to the table.

FRENCH QUARTER
GEM & LAPIDARY

Sparkle and bling

527 Saint Philip Street (between Chartres and Decatur)
+1 504 524 9596   facebook.com/FrenchQuarterGemLapidary
Closed Tuesday

My Nanny Angelina loved jewelry. I'd always bring her treasures from the French Quarter Gem & Lapidary, a shop that has enough glitz to please any magpie. Located on Saint Philip Street, near the French Market, this jewel box serves up everything from fresh water pearls to any gemstone imaginable. This is the place for eye-popping crystals, custom made birthstone jewelry and even the trickiest of delicate repairs. If you're not sure what you want, the friendly and ever-patient staff will show you possibilities you may not have considered. Best of all, reasonable prices will leave you with cash left over to show off your new purchases over lunch.

GREEN GODDESS

Esoteric dining in a charming alley setting

307 Exchange Place (between Conti and Bienville) / +1 504 301 3347
greengoddessrestaurant.com / Closed Monday and Tuesday

Green Goddess is one French Quarter eatery that has nothing to do with this city's traditional culinary past. Adventurous Chef Paul Artigues blows the doors off this tiny place with dishes like his take on shrimp Clemenceau made with local Gulf Shrimp sautéed with onions, tomato and lardons, finished with light cream and a hint of Italian fish sauce. And "notorious" isn't overstating the bacon sundae made with micro-planed Nueske's Applewood bacon over pecan praline ice cream with a creamy bacon caramel sauce. Cocktails are nectar-of-the-gods quality, while the wine list perfectly and poetically matches the menu. Just don't expect a swooning black jacket service experience. The style here is decidely laissez-faire.

KITCHEN WITCH

Cookbooks in all flavors

631 Toulouse Street (between Royal and Chartres)   +1 504 528 8382
kwcookbooks.com   Closed Monday and Tuesday

In a city that loves its grub, this food-focused bookshop is a witty oasis of culinary tomes, infused with both a sense of humor and a selection of highly collectible editions. This is a shop for those who love to cook, read about cooking and talk about cooking. From a rare and coveted book on modernist cuisine to signed first editions of a certain French cookbook by someone named Julia, the well-curated stock bubbles with verve and intelligence. This is also an incredible anthropological library of every Louisianan and New Orleans cookbook ever published. Oh, and don't get me started on their ode to the genre of spiral bound community cookbooks.

LUCULLUS
Haute culinary vintage

610 Chartres Street (between Toulouse and Wilkinson)
+1 504 528 9620 / lucullusantiques.com
Closed Sunday and Monday

At the fascinating Lucullus, the focus is on antique culinaria — the shop sells everything from old china and silver settings to rustic farmhouse implements and accoutrements for the ritualistic serving of absinthe. Lucullus can help you recreate fantasy scenes from *Babette's Feast*, complete with 19th-century copper cookware, a Napoleonic porcelain soup tureen, and eating implements specific to each course. Or there are bright red and yellow 1950s shellfish plates perfect for a Technicolor Bardot and Truffaut picnic on the Riviera — or at least on Lakeshore Drive. Although prices can inspire sticker shock, even the budget-minded can find simple pleasures in vintage café au lait bowls and 1920s cordial glasses.

NOLA KIDS

Great kids toys and duds

333 Chartres Street (between Conti and Bienville) / +1 504 566 1340
shopnolakids.com / Open daily

The oh-so-cute NOLA Kids is my go-to for gifts for the discriminating peanut. Their shopping experience is pure playtime, with a fabulous selection of kids' books that are fun to read, no matter how old you are. Many are New Orleans- and Louisiana-centric, like *Alligator Wedding* and *Grandma's Gumbo*, which might account for the gaggle of grannies I saw shopping there just the other day. There's a pirate rain coat that is Mardi Gras worthy, if only it came in bigger sizes. Adorable stuffed animals, ballerina Topsy Turvy dolls, hip and cool diaper bags, they're all here. As for the line of Noodle & Boo bath products... I'm thinking that's ageless.

QUARTER PAST TIME

Old-style tellers of time

606 Chartres Street (between Toulouse and Wilkinson)
+1 504 410 9010 / facebook.com/pages/Quarter-Past-Time
Closed Wednesday

Care to tango? Whether or not you're in the market for a fab vintage timepiece, walk into Quarter Past Time to meet watch impresario and the shop's owner, Julio Canosa. A true South American-bred gentleman with an air of composed elegance and a mischievous smile, Julio is an expert in rare vintage Omegas, Piagets and Rolexes along with perfectly restored clocks, which he keeps secured in a safe in the back of the store. When I asked which was his pick, a shiny blue and red antique radio was produced. Julio is known to offer tango twirls accompanied by Argentinean music of the soul. Who knows what other special items he harbors in his safe, but one thing is for sure, the man is light on his feet

SYLVAIN

Elegant gastropub

625 Chartres Street (between Saint Peter and Toulouse)
+1 504 265 8123 / sylvainnola.com / Open daily

Owner Sean McCusker told me once that he opened Sylvain because there was nowhere good to eat in the French Quarter. That didn't sit well with me, but I can say there's nothing quite like Sylvain in the neighborhood. The romantic, dimly lit bar and dining room (a former carriage house) benefits from Chef Alex Harrell's sophisticated yet approachable fare, much with a Southern accent, often sourced locally. The pork Milanese with farro and roasted veg, all treated with smoky bacon and onion vinaigrette is but one delicious example. The buttermilk-fried Chick-Syl-vain sandwich is also a must try. To wash it all down, there's an impressive selection of bourbons along with a terrific craft cocktail menu.

NOLA AFTER DARK:
craft cocktail bars

Shaken and stirred

Some say that the cocktail was invented in New Orleans. Whether or not that's true, there is no denying that many a cocktail has been birthed in the Crescent City, undoubtedly the lodestar of American drinking culture.

In recent years, a new generation of innovative mixologists has been playing with venerable tipple traditions, adding new recipes, fresh ingredients, hand-squeezed juices and homemade syrups and tinctures. When I want to worship at the altar of Sazerac, I go to **The Sazerac Bar** in the gorgeous Roosevelt Hotel, where the 19th-century original recipe made with Cognac, Peychaud's bitters and Herbsaint Legendre is favored.

For a frothy Ramos gin fizz, a favorite of notorious past governor Huey P. Long, I like to wander to **Bar Tonique** on Rampart across from Armstrong Park, a chilled neighborhood spot with a superb list of drinks and a daily $5 special. The innovative bar **Cure** was opened by local cocktail pioneers Neal Bodenheimer and Matthew Kohnke in a renovated firehouse on Freret Street long before this uptown corridor was on anybody else's radar.

Although the Pimm's Cup is quintessentially British, **Napoleon House** popularized it locally in a setting that reminds me of Amsterdam's brown cafés. When I need reviving, I head to **SoBou** (South of Bourbon), where head "bar chef" Abigail Deirdre Gullo creates a bracing Corpse Reviver No. 2 made with Cocchi Americano. Ticky tacky tiki is the rage at **Tiki Tolteca** in the Quarter. I like the classic Mai Tai, although the shareable zombie punch is a potent tropical vacation. Over at **Cane & Table**, proto-tiki concoctions made with rum, spices and fruit to mirror local culinary traditions are on the sophisticated drinks menu that pre-dates LA's surf-driven Tiki wave.

For an old school love potion, bartender Chris Hannah at **Arnaud's French 75 Bar** (see pg 52) mixes that namesake drink with Cognac instead of gin. I'd never had a Grasshopper until bartender Brian Kientz poured me the minty dreamsicle at **Tujague's**, a revelatory sip at the bar where it was invented.

BAR TONIQUE
820 North Rampart Street (between Dumaine and
Saint Ann), +1 504 324 6045, bartonique.com, open daily

CANE & TABLE
1113 Decatur Street (at Ursalines), +1 504 581 1112
caneandtablenola.com, open daily

CURE
4905 Freret Street (at Upperline), +1 504 302 2357
curenola.com, open daily

NAPOLEON HOUSE
500 Chartres Street (at St Louis), +1 504 524 9752
napoleonhouse.com, open daily

SOBOU
W Hotel French Quarter, 310 Chartres Street
(between Conti and Bienville), +1 504 552 4095
sobounola.com, open daily

THE SAZERAC BAR
123 Baronne Street (between Canal and Tulane)
+1 504 648 1200, therooseveltneworleans.com/dining/
the-sazerac-bar, open daily

TIKI TOLTECA
301 North Peters Street (at Bienville), +1 504 288 8226
felipestaqueria.com/neworleans/tiki-tolteca, open daily

TUJAGUE'S
823 Decatur Street (at Madison), +1 504 525 8676
tujaguesrestaurant.com, open daily

NOLA AFTER DARK:
live music venues

A culture of groove

Live music is the life force that oxygenates the culture of New Orleans – the city where jazz purportedly was born. I love that I hear live music everywhere, from the buskers on Royal to the uptown juke joints.

It's possible on any night of the week to second line with a brass band along Frenchmen Street, catch a reggae groove at **Cafe Negril** or swing dance at **The Spotted Cat Music Club**. Across the street, it's rootsy rock and brass at **d.b.a**. At **Snug Harbor Jazz Bistro**, old school jazz rules, with patriarch Ellis Marsalis in residence most Friday nights. In Mid-City, bowl a few games before groups playing zydeco, rock or blues take to the stage at the family-owned **Rock 'n' Bowl**. The intimate **Chickie Wah Wah** on Canal draws a slightly older crowd to its acoustic sessions; if you're lucky, Jon Cleary will be at the piano. Uptown, **Tipitina's** (known as Tip's) is legendary; a New Orleans institution since 1977 and a must visit for any music lover. On your way out, give the bust of local pianist Professor Longhair a rub for luck. The **Maple Leaf Bar** on Oak Street is a cab ride from the Quarter but well worth the fare to catch the sassy notes of the renowned Rebirth Brass Band, there most Tuesday nights from around midnight.

Remember that shows never start on time in this town, so relax and settle in. And when the tip jar comes your way, be generous. In a place so rich with great music, musicians are still playing hard to make ends meet.

CAFE NEGRIL
606 Frenchmen Street (at Kerlerec), +1 504 944 4744
frenchmenstreetlive.com/cafe-negril, open daily

CHICKIE WAH WAH
2828 Canal Street (between Canal and Cleveland)
+1 504 304 4714, chickiewahwah.com, open daily

D.B.A.
618 Frenchment Street (between Chartres and Royal)
+1 504 942 3731, dbaneworleans.com, open daily

MAPLE LEAF BAR
8316 Oak Street (between Cabronne and Dante)
+1 504 866 9359, mapleleafbar.com, open daily

ROCK 'N' BOWL
3016 South Carrollton Avenue (at Dublin)
+1 504 861 1700, rocknbowl.com, open daily

SNUG HARBOR JAZZ BISTRO
626 Frenchmen Street (between Chartres and Royal)
+1 504 949 0696, snugjazz.com, open daily

THE SPOTTED CAT MUSIC CLUB
623 Frenchmen Street (between Chartres and Royal)
no phone, spottedcatmusicclub.com, open daily

TIPITINA'S
501 Napoleon Avenue (at Tchoupitoulas)
+1 504 895 8477, tipitinas.com, open daily

mid-city
and treme

Before I lived in New Orleans, the Jazz and Heritage
Festival was the main reason to visit the Bayou
Saint John area of Mid-City, home to the historic
Fairgrounds that hosts my favorite music event.
I would walk along Esplanade Avenue, past the
colorful Creole cottages in historic Treme, and always
just head for the Fest. Now I know better and frequent
Mid-City often, a wide swathe of secondary
neighborhoods including City Park and bustling
Carrollton Avenue. Accessible by car, by bus along
Esplanade Ridge through Treme and by streetcar up
Canal, Mid-City is anchored by the Fairgrounds Race
Course on one end and Carrollton Avenue on the
other. With its colorful mix of architectural styles,
from single shotguns to epic Victorian mansions,
this district attracts artists, single professionals and
families with social pedigrees.

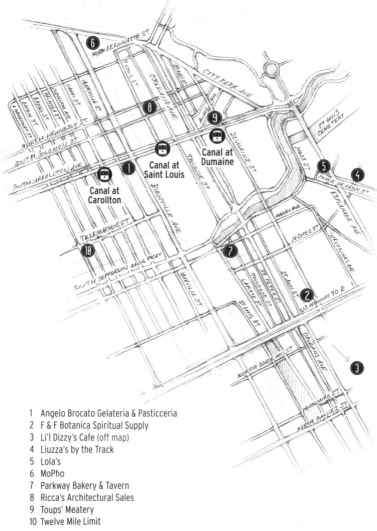

1 Angelo Brocato Gelateria & Pasticceria
2 F & F Botanica Spiritual Supply
3 Li'l Dizzy's Cafe (off map)
4 Liuzza's by the Track
5 Lola's
6 MoPho
7 Parkway Bakery & Tavern
8 Ricca's Architectural Sales
9 Toups' Meatery
10 Twelve Mile Limit

ANGELO BROCATO GELATERIA & PASTICCERIA

Old-fashioned Italian treats

214 North Carrollton Avenue (between Iberville and Bienville)
+1 504 486 0078 / angelobrocatoicecream.com / Closed Monday

When I want to channel the Italian essence of my Aunt Rose, may she rest in peace, I head to Angelo Brocato, a family business that has dished silky gelato and traditional sweets since the turn of last century. On a typical evening, the place is overflowing with families and young couples. Watch as the welcoming young ladies behind the counter expertly pipe to order the ricotta into your cannoli shell. Sip an espresso and order a plate of tiramisu or a slice of house-made cassata cake. As Aunt Rose used to proclaim, "What are you waiting for? Mangia!"

F & F BOTANICA SPIRITUAL SUPPLY

Santeria and Voodoo supplies

801 North Broad Street (corner of Saint Ann) / +1 504 289 2304
orleanscandleco.com / Closed Sunday and Monday

Some Voodoo shops in this city are total tourist traps. It's hard for me
not to laugh when some new age stoner charges $20 for an "authentic
purification ceremony," which means waving a couple of pet snakes around
to synthesized Haitian drum music. But Voodoo (and its cousin Santeria)
is a serious religion, and F & F Botanica Spiritual Supply celebrates this.
Don't worry; it's the furthest thing from scary here. No one will give you the
evil eye, and there are no snakes. The calm and friendly staff will, however,
guide you through the rituals, potions, and tools of this fascinating religion,
which can also be used (i.e., candles, bath salts) in your everyday life.

LI'L DIZZY'S CAFE

Soulful Creole cuisine, family style

1500 Esplanade Avenue (at North Robertson) / +1 504 569 8997
lildizzyscafe.com / Open daily

Fried chicken is one of my favorite breakfast foods, and Li'l Dizzy's Cafe is my favorite place to eat it. Not being an egg person, I especially appreciate the savory options on the belly-busting buffet breakfast/brunch menu at this family owned spot, maybe one of the only places in the city where alcohol doesn't flow. It's more of a homey scene, with lots of table hopping and banter between the regulars. Owner Wayne Baquet's New Orleans roots go back centuries, and his ancestors have a long history in the restaurant business. That Creole filé gumbo you're slurping is made from a family recipe that the Baquets have been serving for decades.

LIUZZA'S BY THE TRACK

Neighborhood pub with great gumbo

1518 North Lopez Street (at Ponce De Leon) / +1 504 218 7888
liuzzasnola.com / Closed Sunday

More often than not, when I pick up pals at the airport I take them
directly to Liuzza's by the Track for the signature barbecue shrimp po-boy.
In a city that's po-boy proud, Liuzza's stands out from the crowd, thanks
to this buttery, Worcestershire-fueled gi-normous portion of gulf shrimp
slathered between a hot and crusty pistolette. You won't find a better
corner pub, and you won't taste a better gumbo, although the oyster
po-boys with garlic butter and the garlic-stuffed beef po-boys with
horseradish go down mighty fine with a cold mug of Abita amber ale.
Just a block from the track, this is always the first stop on the way to
Jazz Fest, the street swarming with music lovers slurping down Liuzza's
eye-poppingly spicy Bloody Marys.

LOLA'S

Spanish comfort food

3312 Esplanade Avenue (between Maurepas and Ponce De Leon)
+1 504 488 6946 / lolasneworleans.com / Open daily

Paella is a gift from the gods, and while I make a pretty mean one myself (in a pan hauled home from Barcelona), Lola's is where I head for this seafood, chorizo and saffron-powered specialty. I order it first thing, or its sister dish fideuà made with pasta, because it takes 30 minutes to prepare, but the upside of that is I have plenty of time to tuck into tapas like garlic mushrooms or crabmeat with avocado in homemade aioli. This tiny family-run place, in strolling distance of Bayou Saint John, is authentically Spanish meets Creole, thanks to the template left by the late Seville-born owner Angel Miranda, and the locally sourced seafood and ingredients.

MOPHO

Modern take on Vietnamese dishes

514 City Park Avenue (between Toulouse and Saint Louis)
+1 504 482 6845 / mophonola.com / Open daily

Vietnamese food has long been a staple here, but you had to travel to
New Orleans East or the West Bank to get it. That's all changed as pho
places are popping up all over now. MoPho stands apart. Chef/owner
Michael Gulotta marries the fresh, fermented pungent goodness of
Vietnamese cuisine with contemporary New Orleans bounty. I adore
the ginger and lemongrass chicken wings and the familiar meets exotic
hot sausage po-boy dressed with bánh mì garnishes. The crispy fried
oysters with pickled blue cheese are a slam dunk, same goes for the
pork belly noodles and pho fragrant with star anise. The craft cocktails
are bracingly good, too.

PARKWAY BAKERY & TAVERN

Old school Nola po-boys

538 Hagan Street (at Toulouse) / **+1 504 482 3047**
parkwaypoorboys.com   Closed Tuesday

When I need my car worked on at R&S Automotive, I schedule it around lunchtime. That's because the garage is across from Parkway Bakery & Tavern, a place that has defined po-boys in New Orleans for the better part of a century. The juicy roast beef po-boy is at least a four-napkiner, "dressed" as it is with lettuce, tomato, mayonnaise, and pickles. A landmark since 1911, some believe this is where the delish "poor boy" sandwich was invented to feed the workers at the American Can Company. Thank goodness neighbor Jay Nix reopened the place in 2003 after a decade of darkness when the original owners closed up shop. Thanks Jay, and pass the napkins.

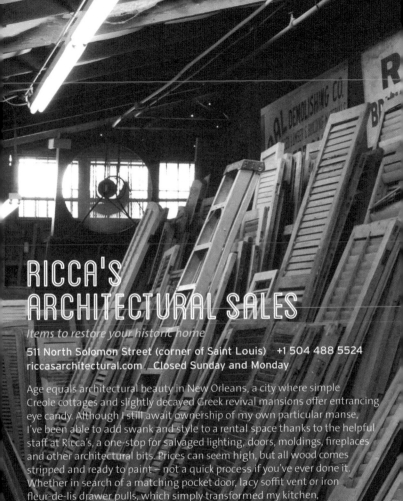

RICCA'S
ARCHITECTURAL SALES

Items to restore your historic home

511 North Solomon Street (corner of Saint Louis)   +1 504 488 5524
riccasarchitectural.com   Closed Sunday and Monday

Age equals architectural beauty in New Orleans, a city where simple
Creole cottages and slightly decayed Greek revival mansions offer entrancing
eye candy. Although I still await ownership of my own particular manse,
I've been able to add swank and style to a rental space thanks to the helpful
staff at Ricca's, a one-stop for salvaged lighting, doors, moldings, fireplaces
and other architectural bits. Prices can seem high, but all wood comes
stripped and ready to paint – not a quick process if you've ever done it.
Whether in search of a matching pocket door, lacy soffit vent or iron
fleur-de-lis drawer pulls, which simply transformed my kitchen,
you'll find it in Ricca's portal back in time.

TOUPS' MEATERY

Carnivore heaven

845 North Carrollton Avenue (at Dumaine) / +1 504 252 4999
toupsmeatery.com / Closed Sunday

When I need a protein fix with panache, I head to Toups' Meatery on Carrollton, Chef Isaac Toups' ode to meat. You might call it contemporary Cajun with flair; what happens when a Cajun boy spends 10 years in fine dining. A dish like braised lamb neck with fennel and pickled mirliton over black-eyed peas is the best of both Creole and Cajun worlds. Start with the meat board, a charcuterie of house-made cured meats and condiments that includes the likes of ginger-lemongrass barbecue meatballs and foie gras torchon with seasonal jam and spiced pecans. There is one green salad on the menu, but really why bother? Eat your veggies elsewhere and tuck into boldly flavored, slow cooked, grilled and barbecued goodness.

TWELVE MILE LIMIT

Expert tipples on the cheap

500 South Telemachus Street (at Baudin) / +1 504 488 8114
facebook.com/twelve.mile.limit / Closed Monday

Take an honest-to-goodness neighborhood dive bar, a vintage juke box
and add craft cocktails at rock bottom prices, and you wind up with
Twelve Mile Limit. T. Cole Newton — one of the city's top bartenders — owns
the joint, which features a smokin' barbecue kitchen and tasty drinks. I can
get a French 75 here, in my preferred kind of stemware, a coupe glass, for $7.
And that's not well brand gin. I love this place for bringing high-brow booze
to a dog friendly setting without an ounce of pretense. Quirky theme
nights — board games, trivia, old school dance parties — add élan to the no
frills setting. Newton began his bartending career at high-end restaurants
Coquette and Commander's Palace, so aren't we lucky? Yes, I'll have another.

outdoor oases

Inviting green spaces

AUDUBON PARK
6500 Magazine Street (between Saint Charles Avenue
and the river), +1 504 861 2537
auduboninstitute.org/audubon-park, open daily

CITY PARK
Palm Drive (Esplanade and City Park Avenue)
+1 504 482 4888, neworleanscitypark.com, open daily

CRESCENT PARK
North Peters Street (between Montegut and Alvar)
+1 504 658 4000, nola.gov/city/crescent-park, open daily

LAKESHORE DRIVE
Lakeshore Drive (at Elysian Fields), open daily

Sure, we proud residents of New Orleans love to indulge and party into the wee hours. But thankfully, when we need to air ourselves out, there are plenty of green and leafy places to help us commune with nature.

City Park is a 1,300 acre Eden with striking stands of live oak trees and an endless array of outdoor recreation facilities. I like to walk my dog Ruby around the manmade lake in search of frogs and yellow-footed egrets. There's a gondola for hire, piloted by a Cajun guy who learned the trade in Venice. And there's the New Orleans Museum of Art, with its free outdoor sculpture garden for strolling, and nearby a still-working antique carousel and a play area for kids.

Before or after a visit to the recently expanded Audubon Zoo, have a picnic in **Audubon Park**, a former plantation sandwiched between the river and Saint Charles Avenue. Shaded by giant live oaks and ancient magnolias, the 400-acre space offers jogging, hiking and biking trails. Ask a local to direct you to The Fly, a section of the park that is a beehive of activity. Everything that's fun happens here: from barbecues to Frisbee throws and soccer games. As it follows the levee, it's also a great spot for watching the Mississippi river traffic; an endless flow of commercial barges and ships from exotic ports of call.

The newest kid on the green block is **Crescent Park,** a 1.4-mile span from Elysian Fields Avenue in the Marigny to Mazant Street in Bywater; notable for its rusted Piety Street pedestrian bridge arching over the active railroad tracks below. Pathways, planted with indigenous foliage, offer a spectacular city skyline view.

For relaxing sunset views of vast Lake Pontchartrain, I love to bring an adult beverage and sit along the lake front on **Lakeshore Drive**. It's not uncommon to see pelicans and picnickers from the benches that line the lake.

the cbd and warehouse district

Neighborhood boundaries in this city sometimes seem as fluid as the Mississippi River. Canal Street, which runs from the river to the lake, historically divided the French from the more affluent – and Southern – American sector. Today Canal is the gateway to the Central Business District (CBD).

If you're in the Quarter and lose orientation, just look for what passes as a skyline here: the outline of the convention hotels and the office buildings along Poydras signal that you're heading uptown.

The Warehouse District is another area in flux. Having once stored the bounty that made New Orleans the richest city in America, the buildings were abandoned and blighted just a few decades ago. Now this area is home to a concentration of arts organizations and museums, loft residences and an increasing number of film production companies and sound stages.

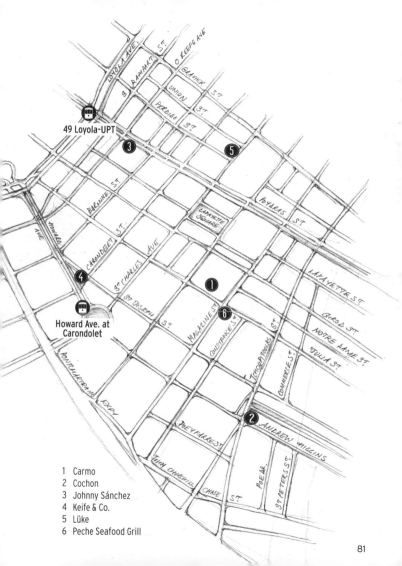

49 Loyola-UPT

Howard Ave. at
Carondolet

1 Carmo
2 Cochon
3 Johnny Sánchez
4 Keife & Co.
5 Lüke
6 Peche Seafood Grill

CARMO

Healthy and delicious

527 Julia Street (between Camp and Magazine) / +1 504 875 4132
cafecarmo.com / Closed Sunday

When raw food fanatic Woody Harrelson is in town shooting a movie,
he gets all of his chow from Carmo, the only restaurant in Louisiana
certified by the Green Restaurant Association. An oasis of fresh, local
ingredients, with an emphasis on vegetarian and vegan fare, along with
sustainable seafood and other options for omnivores, Carmo makes healthy
delicious. It's my go-to when I want to eat out, but can't bear the thought
of another piece of fried food doused in heavy sauces. Also, if you care
about consuming humanely raised meats, organic non-gmo soy and corn
products, gluten-free everything and food that is locally sourced this is the
place for you.

COCHON

Modern Cajun

930 Tchoupitoulas Street (corner of Andrew Higgins)
+1 504 588 2123 / cochonrestaurant.com / Closed Sunday

Chef-owner Donald Link pays homage to all things porcine at this inspired Cajun restaurant with a serious moonshine list. His German-Acadian roots are evident in dishes such as fried boudin with pickled peppers, pork-and-black-eyed-pea gumbo and delectable fried chicken livers with pepper-jelly toast. I've eaten here dozens of times and have had nothing but fantastic meals. True country Cajuns — who are known for being a little bit crazy — will eat just about anything, including those swamp rodents known as nutria, and they will make it delectable. Cochon features modern and more mainstream Cajun dishes such as the namesake roasted cochon with crackling, which proves even down-home country food can get gussied up real nice when in deft hands.

JOHNNY SÁNCHEZ

Stylish Mexican on Poydras

930 Poydras Street (at O'Keefe) / **+1 504 304 6615**
johnnysanchezrestaurant.com / **Open daily**

I can't stop thinking about the sprouts, yes Brussels sprouts, fried and made into a salad with bits of roasted squash, pomegranate and queso... The Mexican love child of local über-chef John Besh and Food Network wunderkind Aarón Sánchez, Johnny Sánchez is locally charged and full of authentic Mexican flavors. The pork belly tacos are sweetened with pineapple glaze, and are savory with swine-y goodness. The lamb enchiladas are delicious, as are the yellowtail tostados, slow-roasted mole — and just about every darn thing on the menu. There are some interesting (and pricey) wines by the glass, along with a very good house margarita and a full list of sipping tequilas. The place also happens to be gorgeous, with colorful Day of the Dead mural art and Chihuly-style overhead chandeliers.

KEIFE & CO.

European-type wine and cheese shop

801 Howard Avenue (at Corondolet) / +1 504 523 7272
keifeandco.com / Closed Sunday and Monday

Attentive service, soaring ceilings and library shelves filled with smartly selected bottles make this neighborhood store anything but ordinary. The hand-picked wine collection runs the gamut from a truly impressive $15 bottle of Camino de Navaherreros Garnacha from Spain for everyday drinking to a triple-digit priced vintage Burgundy. Most producers are small boutique owner/vintners with an emphasis on organic and natural viticulture. Co-owner Jim Yonkus oversees the rockin' cheese selection, along with imported charcuterie and the likes of caviar, exotic preserves and pickles, Parisian caramels and artisanal olive oils and vinegars. This is where I go when I'm looking for a host/hostess gift sure to impress.

LÜKE

Brasserie meets bayou

333 Saint Charles Avenue (corner of Perdido) / +1 504 378 2840
lukeneworleans.com / Open daily

Lüke, a John Besh winner named after his eldest son, is a bustling Franco-German brasserie, the kind of place that used to be common in New Orleans back in the day. A handsome space defined by a beautiful, carved-wood bar, Lüke offers a daily special such as roasted suckling pig, duck cassoulet or braised beef short ribs. The Alsatian dishes like the jägerschnitzel mit spätzle (fried veal cutlets) accompanied by wild mushrooms are especially memorable. This place also has one of the best oyster happy hour deals in the city, which makes it my ideal stop on the way to the Superdome.

PECHE SEAFOOD GRILL

Local taste of the sea

800 Magazine Street (between Julia and Saint Joseph)
+1 504 522 1744 / pecherestaurant.com / Closed Sunday

With the same singular focus they apply to pork at Cochon, chef/
partners Donald Link and Stephen Stryjewski hone in on all things
seafood at this industrial chic Warehouse District eatery. This restaurant
is all about local and line-caught, most of it cooked on an epic hardwood
fire grill. Chef/partner Ryan Prewitt delivers intriguing dishes like spicy
Asian-flavored capellini with crab and chilies, beer battered fish sticks
and some of the most delicious grilled whole redfish you'll ever eat in
your life, a rustic beauty flavored with a lemony salsa verde. The menu
changes frequently and the place is extremely popular, so reserve early.

the garden district

Taking the streetcar up Saint Charles to go
rambling through the Garden District and along
Magazine Street is one of the great pleasures to
be had in New Orleans. Leafy and green,
this residential swathe, like much of the city, was
originally the site of a plantation. But while the
Quarter and the Marigny retained their French
and Creole roots, the Garden District was part of
the American sector, and back in the day,
the cultural divide was vast, with very distinct
style and customs in both areas. I can only
imagine the fortunes made on Mississippi river
trade as I gawk at turreted Victorians, Italianate
and Greek Revival manses along streets like
Washington, Saint Charles and Prytania.

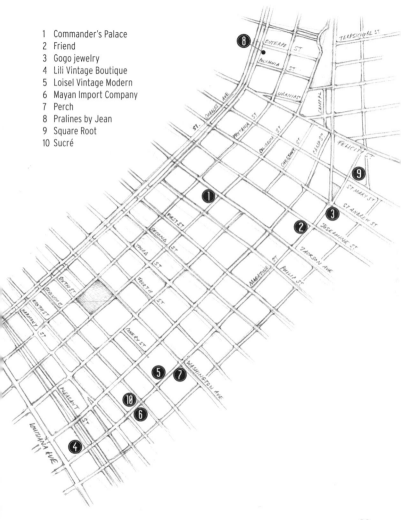

1 Commander's Palace
2 Friend
3 Gogo jewelry
4 Lili Vintage Boutique
5 Loisel Vintage Modern
6 Mayan Import Company
7 Perch
8 Pralines by Jean
9 Square Root
10 Sucré

COMMANDER'S PALACE

Antebellum history, flawless service and clever classic cuisine

1403 Washington Avenue (corner of Coliseum) / +1 504 899 8221
commanderspalace.com / Open daily

The very sight of the green and white awning at Commander's Palace gets my stomach rumbling. Hailed by tourists, beloved by locals, the circa-1880 grande dame of the Garden District is where celebrity chefs Emeril Lagasse and Paul Prudhomme started out, and the Brennan family has maintained a tradition of culinary excellence since 1969. Chef Tory McPhail, a James Beard award winner, keeps the emphasis squarely on local produce, seafood and game. The list of wines by the glass is epic, with at least 45 options available, as well as half bottles, an oenophile's dream. Weekend jazz brunch is a must, complete with Bloody Marys, Eggs Sardou and excellent bread pudding, but don't miss the 25-cent martinis at lunch Monday to Friday either.

FRIEND

Easy style for men

2115 Magazine Street (between Josephine and Jackson)
+1 504 218 4214 / friendneworleans.com / Open daily

When it comes to everyday fashion, my guy friends tend to be jeans and T-shirts types, but perusing the racks at Friend, I am tempted to ask them to up their style stakes. The look is classic resort-meets-surf/skate sensibility, a combo that is softly tailored and unfussy. Owner Parker Hutchinson, a musician-turned-lawyer-turned-shopkeeper, sells the kind of clothes he likes to wear himself: stylish and affordable brands such as Saturdays, A.P.C., Our Legacy, 18 Waits, Vanishing Elephant and Shades of Grey. I especially appreciate his collaboration with local artists and designers ranging from perfume oil by Kathleen Currie to backpacks by Patti Dunn and products by green friendly Tchoup Industries.

GOGO JEWELRY

Power punk jewelry designs

2036 Magazine Street (between Josephine and Saint Andrew)
+1 504 529 8868   ilovegogojewelry.com   Closed Sunday and Monday

There are plenty of arty jewelry designers in this town selling fleur-de-lis pendants – which I love, and I have several – but for the times when you want to make a right-now statement, there's the groovily named Gogo Borgerding, a designer who creates eye-popping jewelry with necklaces that say "POW" and bracelets that Wonder Woman might wear. Her store sells not only her bold pieces, but also features other talented and sometimes unknown jewelers' creations. Some of the pieces are Louisiana-inspired, like the nubby crawfish claw pendants in silver or bronze and hand cut sterling shadowboxes replicating the gas lights that flicker outside many a French Quarter cottage.

LILI VINTAGE BOUTIQUE

Clothes that make a statement

3329 Magazine Street (between Louisiana and Toledano)
+1 504 931 6848 / lilivintage.com / Open daily

There isn't a way you're supposed to dress in free-spirited New Orleans.
I often forget that other cities don't follow suit, and have wound up in
places like Philadelphia with a case full of tulle and sequins. That leads
me to think of Lili Vintage Boutique; a shop that makes its own rules.
A repository of chic, this is your place, whether you're seeking 1930s
skirts or sheer slip dresses straight from *A Streetcar Named Desire*.
Lili isn't just an average vintage store — it's a store for clothing collectors,
eccentric and otherwise; for people who feel that it's perfectly
acceptable to wear rhinestones with 1960s chiffon to buy groceries,
should you please. That's why I love it.

LOISEL VINTAGE MODERN

Mid-century chic

2855 Magazine Street (at Sixth) / +1 504 899 2444
loiselvintagemodern.squarespace.com / Open daily

In a city obsessed with history and antiques, Loisel Vintage Modern is a
bracing slap in the face. The "futuristic" design of furniture in the 1950s
is something I first discovered while visiting my dad in Palm Springs,
a desert city known for its mid-20th-century design sensibility. The less
is more approach is the antithesis of fusty, and I appreciate mixing
in a piece here and there with my other shabby chic furnishings.
Owner Vic Loisel's trained eye has brought together a fine line of vintage
furniture, lamps and housewares from the 1940s to the 1970s. The
designs are straightforward, the lines are clean and the effect is timeless.

MAYAN IMPORT COMPANY

Cigars with savoir faire

3000 Magazine Street (between Seventh and Eighth)
+1 504 269 9000 / bigeasytobacconist.com / Open daily

Set inside an old, imposing orphanage building on Magazine Street,
Mayan Import Company has a couple of tables out front in the shade
where you can sit and puff on your stogies as you watch people
walking by. The well informed staff will help you choose your smoke of
choice from an impressive selection of cigars, cigarettes and tobaccos,
and you can also browse almost every piece of 20th-century literature
that speaks to blowing smoke. Yes, this is the place to come for a
Romeo Y Julieta or a few ounces of Norwegian Shag – if you
can keep a straight face while ordering it.

PERCH

Antique and contemporary home stuff

2844 Magazine Street (between Sixth and Washington)
+1 504 899 2122 / perch-home.com / Closed Sunday

One of my favorite stops on Magazine Street, Perch is a repository of
inspired home accessories and furnishings that drip eclectic style.
Housed in an airy 1860s double shotgun, the shop is a mix of modern
paired with carefully chosen antiques and whimsical vintage. A design
team is on hand to offer advice if you're more of a DIY type. The stock
changes frequently, with recent bestsellers ranging from colorful wall-
mounted papier mâché animal heads to boldly hued accent cushions and
plastic tumblers in 13 shades. This is a super spot to shop for engagement
and wedding gifts if you're not prone to following the registry.

PRALINES BY JEAN

Quality confectionery and cupcakes too

1728 Saint Charles Avenue (corner of Polymnia) / +1 504 525 1910
pralinesbyjean.com / Closed Sunday

If it's a toothsome New Orleans-centric treat you're seeking to stash in
your carry on, pecan pralines are the bomb. Pronounced PRAAW-leans,
not PRAY-leens if you're trying to speak local, these achingly sweet
confections hark back to the age when sugar plantations lined the
Mississippi and the export of cane sugar made millionaires. I'm more of a
savory girl myself, but I've found that a box of pralines by Jean is a real door
opener. Made from butter, brown sugar, cream and pecans, you can also
find them flavored with chocolate, peanut butter, coconut or rum. These
beauties are made fresh daily, as are the cupcakes that are also for sale.

SQUARE ROOT

Art meets science on a plate

1800 Magazine Street (between Felicity and Saint Mary)
+1 504 309 7800 / squarerootnola.com   Closed Sunday and Monday

I wasn't exactly sure what "roasted coco caraway gravel" referred to on my gorgeously composed plate – liquid nitrogen created a cloud of mystery around ingredients being foamed, frozen and turned into dust – but I knew the flavor was flat out delicious. Square Root is a 16-seat chef's table from force of nature Chef/co-owner Phillip Lopez, whose first eatery, Root, is in the Warehouse District. Square Root is a trailblazer in Nola; avant-garde cooking at the intersection of art and science. The chef visits companionably and shares back-stories as he serves Southern Picnic on a plate, fried chicken paired with pickled fried okra or Eggs Sardou topped with a duck egg yolk and truffle. Have a drink on the balcony at the upstairs bar, Root2.

SUCRÉ

Smart little sweets shop

3025 Magazine Street (corner of Seventh)   +1 504 520 8311
shopsucre.com / Open daily

Headed by Tariq Hanna, pastry chef extraordinaire, Sucré is a sweet
retreat filled with Rome-worthy gelatos and chocolates that stand up
to the finest in Belgium. The macarons are Parisian perfect with delicate
gossamer meringue shells over New Orleans mousseline flavors such
as chicory chocolate or praline. Carnival specialties are legendary,
from a Creole cream cheese filled King Cake to dark chocolate filled
with bananas foster cream and stamped with a gold Mardi Gras mask.
If it's confections and tea you're craving toddle over to Salon by Sucré,
their tea room in the French Quarter, which is dangerously close to
where I'm sitting right now.

touring the big easy
Wanders and rambles

CONFEDERACY OF CRUISERS
634 Elysian Fields Avenue (at Royal), +1 504 400 5468
confederacyofcruisers.com, daily

DESTINATION KITCHEN FOOD TOURS
915 Dublin Street (between Burthe and Freret)
+1 855 353 6634, destination-kitchen.com, daily

FREE TOURS BY FOOT
2613 Laurel Street (between Third and Fourth)
+1 504 222 2967, freetoursbyfoot.com, daily

HAUNTED HISTORY TOURS
723 Saint Peter Street (between Bourbin and Royal)
+1 888 644 6787, hauntedhistorytours.com, daily

HISTORIC NEW ORLEANS COLLECTION
533 Royal Street (at Toulouse), +1 504 523 4662
hnoc.org, closed Monday

Full disclosure, I'm a tour junkie. I love to explore a new place through the eyes of a savvy guide with a point of view; be it on foot, bicycle or bus. New Orleans delivers super tour options, from a cheesy-fun ghost tour to a neighborhood foodie bike adventure and a tippling trot about town.

If you're not scared of ghosts, explore the shady side of the Vieux Carré with **Haunted History Tours**, which also offer treks to an above ground cemetery for lessons in Big Easy burial customs and a gander at Voodoo Priestess Marie Laveau's final resting place. (Or is it?)

Too often, visitors fail to explore Nola's neighborhoods. Change that with a bike tour offered by **Confederacy of Cruisers**. Options include Creole New Orleans and Cocktail New Orleans, or you can opt for either an exploration of the Ninth Ward or a pedal-powered culinary jaunt that recently had me munching praline bacon at Elizabeth's in Bywater. Guaranteed you'll learn tons about the history, culture and quirks of the city as you roll.

Exploring the architectural topography of the different areas reveals the unique housing styles of shotgun, double shotgun, center hall, side hall, camelback and Creole cottages. **The Historic New Orleans Collection** offers a 45-minute tour that is a prism through which the history of French Quarter architecture, courtyards and styles is illuminated.

Destination Kitchen Food Tours will take you on story-filled strolls along Saint Charles Avenue, with insightful commentary offered in English, French or Spanish, the three languages spoken here for centuries.

Not sure what your budget is? Contact **Free Tours by Foot**, a name-your-own-price walking tour experience where, if you're not happy, there's no need to tip the guide. Tours are by neighborhood – the Quarter, Garden District; or by theme – food and ghosts.

uptown

jefferson to louisiana

In New Orleans, 'Uptown' is an umbrella term that means everything flowing against the river's tide up from Canal Street, embracing the Garden District, Irish Channel, Riverbend and Carrollton neighborhoods. I've always been more of a downtown girl, so learning the nuances of the many 'hoods up river is a gradual process. Magazine Street is a commercial thread that runs through it all. Between Louisiana and Jefferson, the section of Uptown adjacent to the Garden District, is where some of my most-loved restaurants and shops reside. In general the homes become grander the farther they are from the river; the closer, more modest abodes were built to house the folks who worked the river, but didn't get rich off of it.

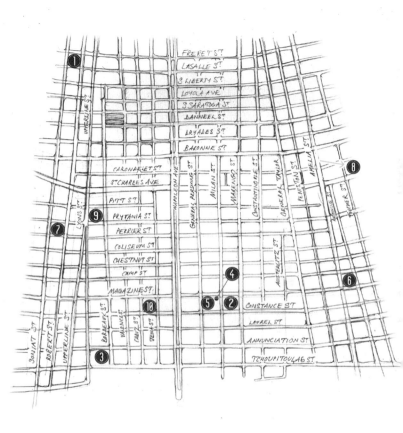

1. Dat Dog
2. Feet First
3. Hansen's Sno-Bliz
4. Ignatius Eatery
5. La Petite Grocery

6. Lilette
7. St. James Cheese Company
8. The Delachaise (off map)
9. Upperline Restaurant
10. Zen Pet Retail & Grooming

DAT DOG

A temple of the wiener

5030 Freret Street (between Soniat and Robert) / +1 504 899 6883
datdognola.com / Open daily

The famous Lucky Dog vendors have been touring the French Quarter
for years, although their wares aren't famous for being tasty, just
gullet-filling. Not so at Dat Dog. Founded in 2011 by a local who made it
big as "the hot dog king of England", this place attracts folks from all over
to sample the best in international sausagery. Now with several locations
in the city, this cash-only eatery delivers the goods. Whether you want the
snap of a classic beef hot dog or the novelty of a wiener fashioned out of
crawfish and smothered with crawfish étouffée, Dat Dog has you covered.
This, the original Freret Street shop is notable for its Technicolor paint job
adorned with whimsical wieners.

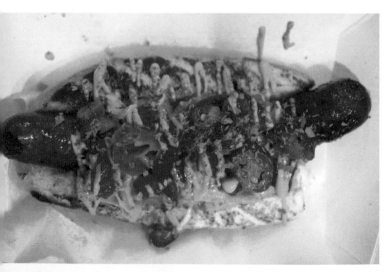

FEET FIRST

Paradise of soles

4122 Magazine Street (between Marengo and Milan)
+1 504 899 6800 / feetfirststores.com / Open daily

Ladies, I know I'm not alone in my obsession with shoes. A new pair
of strappy sandals, sexy stacked heels or butchy motorcycle boots
can transform a bad day into hearts and flowers with the drop of
a credit card. Feet First is the place to go for footwear you won't see
on the masses. In business since 1977, this family-owned retailer
has more than 50 footwear lines for perusal, with names like
Sam Edelman and Pelle Moda on display, along with a slew of
accessories and clothing. When I need a pair of London Fly ankle
strap wedges in pewter, this is where I go.

HANSEN'S SNO-BLIZ

Heavenly frosted goodness

4801 Tchoupitoulis Street (corner of Bordeaux) / +1 504 891 9788
snobliz.com / Open May to August, closed Monday

New Orleans sno-balls are to sno-cones what Degas is to paint-by-
number ballerinas. No mere flavoring of crudely crushed ice, sno-balls
are more like the shaved ice popular in Hawaii. It was Ernest and
Mary Hansen who pioneered the treat with Ernest's patented Sno-Bliz
machine back in 1939. Mary dreamed up endless flavors made from
simple syrups, fruit and condensed milk or whipped cream. Now in
the hands of granddaughter Ashley Hansen, the stand is a hallmark
of imaginative combinations and superior quality perfected by
three generations. Families, hipsters, local dock workers – Hansen's
crowd is always diverse and appreciative. As to my personal pick,
it's the Brown Pelican, a cream of root beer that chills me to the bone.

IGNATIUS EATERY

Down home Creole

3121 Magazine Street (between Eighth and Ninth) / **+1 504 896 0242**
ignatiuseatery.com   Open daily

If Ignatius J. Reilly, deluded anti-hero from *A Confederacy of Dunces*, could dine at the eatery named in his honor, the big slob would find plenty of reasons to swoon. Fried green tomato salad, shrimp and grits, roast beef po-boy, crawfish étouffée, are just a few of the rib-sticking specialties on offer. Ignatius Eatery gets it right in an old school, charming setting, delivering simple, straight-to-the-point New Orleans cooking without a hint of pretense. I especially love the $2 martinis served weekdays from 11am to 6:30pm, and the trio of cochon de lait sliders that go for $6 during happy hour. The restaurant's tagline, "where the locals eat" is the darn truth.

LA PETITE GROCERY

Chic café

4238 Magazine Street (corner of General Pershing)
+1 504 891 3377 / lapetitegrocery.com / Closed Sunday and Monday

When I'm trying to impress my date with a leisurely evening in a romantic setting, the kind of place where whispered sweet nothings can actually be heard, I head to La Petite Grocery. Chef Justin Devillier and his wife Mia are the creative duo behind this shrine to reimagined bistro cooking, with a menu that tempts with the likes of airy ricotta dumplings paired with earthy hen of the woods mushrooms, paneed rabbit with spätzle, and turtle bolognese topped with a fried soft boiled egg. This place is very New Orleans Uptown, not in a crusty old money sense but in a pared down, contemporary way.

LILETTE

The perfect little bistro

3637 Magazine Street (between Louisiana and Napoleon)
+1 504 895 1636 / liletterestaurant.com / Closed Sunday

Created by talented chef-owner John Harris, this classic New Orleans bistro is très romantique, with its stylish toffee-and-cream interior and intimate lighting. While much of the menu is modern French, I especially adore the chef's take on Italian dishes: his version of traditional wedding soup spotlights spinach instead of escarole, with its rich chicken broth floating with tender orbs of veal and pork. The potato gnocchi with sage brown butter and parmigiano cream is awesome as well, but it's tough not to order the steak frites larded with Bordelaise. Pastry chef Carrie Laird's desserts are a must – try the brown butter cake with satsumas alongside a glass of Vin Santo. Perfect for date night, Lilette is modern and unstuffy.

ST. JAMES CHEESE COMPANY

Rare artisanal cheeses, outstanding charcuterie, inspired sandwiches

5004 Prytania Street (between Robert and Soniat) / +1 504 899 4737
stjamescheese.com / Open daily

This pungent fromagerie shop and café easily compares to some of my favorites in Europe. The owners left the corporate world to work in a famed London cheese shop, and then returned to New Orleans to open St. James Cheese Company a year after Katrina. A lovely place to meet friends over house-made charcuterie and dairy delights, St. James also serves an oozingly good Croque Monsieur topped with a brûléed crème fraîche cheese sauce. Yes, more cheese on my cheese sandwich please. Take home more from shelves organized by place of origin, with the helpful counter staff always ready to suggest pairings. When they plunge a knife into a perfectly ripe imported Camembert, I actually feel my knees go weak.

THE DELACHAISE

Vino and nibbles on the Avenue

3442 Saint Charles Avenue (at Delachaise) / +1 504 895 0858
thedelachaise.com / Open daily

My friend Sandie has given me many gifts, but introducing me to
The Delachaise is one of the best. This spirited wine bar is around the
corner from her old house, so was a natural spot for us to meet for vin
and apps. Sandie's long skipped out of town, but I fell in love with this
place for its convivial bar, lack of pretense, kick-ass wine list and, most
notably, the Thai spiced mussels served with goose fat fries. Really,
everything at this atmospheric French-ish bistro is good, but say yes to
the house-made pâté and tender flank steak bruschetta, and double yes
to the devilish chocolate soufflé. Bonus: I can get Viognier and Gruner by
the glass – a treat for this Chardonnay-weary white-wine drinker.

UPPERLINE RESTAURANT

Eclectic French Creole cooking

1413 Upperline Street (corner of Prytania) / +1 504 891 9822
upperline.com / Closed Monday and Tuesday

Owner JoAnn Clevenger makes everyone feel right at home at her cozy Upperline Restaurant, located in a restored 19th-century home brimming with local art. Chef Trent Osborne took over the kitchen in December 2014, and is hitting just the right balance between respecting the timeless dishes that regulars crave and bringing new inspired creations to the table. The drum fish piquant with hot and hot shrimp will never leave the menu, same for the slow roasted half duckling with garlic port sauce. But you might find something like tempura baby eggplant smothered in ginger "barbecue" blue crab as a special, a sign that this uptown spot is always interesting.

ZEN PET RETAIL & GROOMING

Pampering the enlightened pup

4500 Magazine Street, Suite 5 (at Jena)   +1 504 301 4736
zenpetnola.com   Open daily

Ruby has my number. She knows that whenever I travel, I always bring her home a treat, toy or some other bit of fun to make the homecoming that much more special. If you do the same, you'll love Zen Pet Retail & Grooming, a shop and doggie spa that stocks a wide array of natural yummies for your canine pal. Choose from Nola-themed leashes and collars, chew toys and even natural bath products for grooming and gussying. You can also get a doggie fix from Cassie, the resident chocolate lab who greets you at the door. All of the toys for sale are Cassie-approved, in case you were wondering.

where to costume up

Welcome to fantasyland

I've always played dress up. As a little girl, I'd prance around in high heels, pretending to smoke, a feather boa trailing behind me. I still do exactly the same thing, except now I've got company. In this city, a place where costume shops are as common as family-owned grocery stores, there is always a reason to dress up.

Uptown Costume and Dancewear on Magazine Street is quite simply one of the most comprehensive costumers around. Jam-packed with wigs, hats, masks, glitter lashes, boas and costumes of all ilk, this place deserves to be a first stop.

If you want a wow rental, **Southern Costume Company** in the CBD is the bomb. They work with movie companies constantly, but anybody can rent an elaborate getup. You can also buy standards like monsters, naughty nurses and all the necessary accessories.

BUFFALO EXCHANGE
3312 Magazine Street (between Louisiana and Toledano), +1 504 891 7443, buffaloexchange.com
open daily

FUNKY MONKEY
3127 Magazine Street (at Ninth), +1 504 899 5587
facebook.com/FunkyMonkeyNewOrleans, open daily

NEW ORLEANS PARTY AND COSTUME SHOP
705 Camp Street (between Girod and Julia)
+1 504 525 4744, partyandcostume.com, closed Sunday

SOUTHERN COSTUME COMPANY
951 Lafayette Street (between South Rampart and Baronne), +1 504 523 4333, sccnola.com
closed Saturday and Sunday

UPTOWN COSTUME AND DANCEWEAR
4326 Magazine Street (between Napoleon and General Pershing), +1 504 895 7669, uptowncostume.com
open daily

Even when I don't know what I want to be, the knowledgeable staff at **New Orleans Party and Costume Shop** give me plenty of options. This CBD boutique is full of wonders – also a great place if you are in need of rainbow facial hair.

Funky Monkey stocks intriguing duds year-round, but come Mardi Gras, it's in its element. From vintage carnival attire to majorette costumes, sequined band jackets, headpieces and flapper dresses, it's all here.

A country-wide resale boutique that supplies my regular wardrobe year-round, **Buffalo Exchange** in this city also has a costume section, outrageous shoe options and sparkly numbers that are just made for playing dress up.

uptown

jefferson to riverbend

Uptown, above Jefferson towards Riverbend and Carrollton, accessible by the Saint Charles Avenue streetcar that has been rattling along towards the Mississippi for 150 years, is a lively Mecca of college students and high society. Some of the multi-room mansions have been divided into apartments, so it's not unheard of for a collection of hipsters and yuppies to reside next door to an old money clan. It's fun to wander along Oak Street, home to the annual Po-Boy Festival, and a smattering of independent restaurants and shops. Audubon Park (see pg 116), which houses the city's zoo, is also where locals come to walk, run, cycle and barbecue at The Fly, a green space along the levee facing the river.

1 Angelique
2 Boucherie
3 Clancy's
4 Maple Street Patisserie
5 Patois
6 Pied Nu
7 Plum
8 Scriptura

ANGELIQUE

Classic uptown style

7725 Maple Street (between Burdette and Adams) / +1 504 866 1092
angeliquestores.com/boutique.html / Closed Sunday

Some women can effortlessly throw on jeans along with a lacy chiffon blouse and certain je ne sais quoi accessories and look as put-together as a model on the cover of French *Vogue*. I am not one of those women. Thankfully, the stylish lassies at Angelique are ready to help with a selection of great clothing, from both top fashion houses and obscure indie designers. Many of the options are sophisticated in a Jackie O kind of way, but for us funkier types, there are peek-a-boo cut outs and sassy lace numbers that don't need to stay uptown. There's a timeless nature to the clothing here — your purchases will look as fresh in five years as they will this season.

BOUCHERIE

Contemporary Southern

1506 South Carrollton (between Jeannette and Birch)
+1 504 862 5514 / boucherie-nola.com / Closed Sunday and Monday

Modern Southern fare is the dish at this locals' fave set in residential
Carrollton, near where the streetcars retire at night. A February 2015
expansion gave Chef Nathanial Zimet 17 more seats and a waiting area;
much needed space for this smartly casual spot that is always crowded
with regulars who line up for Nathanial's collard greens cooked in a rich
duck stock flavored with garlic, butter and pepper vinegar. Then there's
his intense smoked Wagyu beef brisket served with garlicky parmesan
fries and the decadent Krispy Kreme bread pudding. This is food with
both heart and soul.

CLANCY'S

Hallowed temple of Creole cuisine

6100 Annunciation Street (at Webster) / +1 504 895 1111
clancysneworleans.com / Closed Sunday

Tucked away in residential Uptown, this family-owned traditional Creole restaurant oozes old-style Nola charm. The former bar and po-boy shop has been a white tablecloth eatery since the 1980s, a stalwart for locals who want a Galatoire's experience without crossing Napolean, never mind Canal Street. The ambiance in this timeless culinary landmark is relaxed, and the crowd is loud and lively. I adore the fried oysters with brie, the divine smoked softshell crab piled high with crabmeat is legend and the zippy étouffée bursts with tender local seafood. The voluminous wine list is one of the greatest in town.

MAPLE STREET PATISSERIE

European quality buttery goodness

7638 Maple Street (between Adamas and Hillary)   **+1 504 304 1526**
cargocollective.com/maplestreetpatisserie / **Closed Monday**

Maple Street Patisserie gets its customers the old-fashioned way: they woo them one tasty crumb at a time. Forget about social media and a flashy website, this sweet shop relies on word of mouth fueled by the crazy good skills of the co-owner, a European master baker with old school experience attested to by his flour-dusted hair. The perfect combination of lightness and quality ingredients, the ham and cheese croissant is a savory wonder. Then there's the best slice of apple strudel this side of the Austro-Hungarian Empire. And let's not forget the ethereal towering wedding cakes they make or crumbly seasonal fruit mille feuilles. What a delight.

PATOIS
French cuisine with a local accent

6078 Laurel Street (corner of Webster) / +1 504 895 9441
patoisnola.com / Closed Monday and Tuesday

Kissed by the bright flavors of the Mediterranean and dredged in
the wonder of Southern comfort cuisine, this comely neighborhood
bistro is wattaged by the culinary inspiration of a native son, Chef
Aaron Burgau. The focus is on regional produce, so those are local
chilis spiking the grilled octopus, and that rabbit stuffed with
boudin and wrapped in crispy chicken skin was hopping not long
ago in Mississippi. And the bread I couldn't stop dipping in my spicy
cioppino was baked at Bellegarde on Toledano. It's all so delicious
that I can never bear to leave; instead I soak up more cocktails and
the retro lounge scene in the fab bar.

PIED NU

Barefoot elegance

5521 Magazine Street (corner of Octavia) / +1 504 899 4118
piednunola.com / Closed Sunday

Pied nu is French for barefoot, and when it comes to this place, that bare foot is attached to somebody with tons of effortless style — say a Catherine Deneuve or Juliette Binoche type. The shop pops with personality and a distinctive sensibility that is at once classic and modern. Expect a mix of high-end designer duds and accessories ($635 wide lapel blazer by Áeron, $545 yak bag by Jamin Puech) with reasonably priced gift items sure to impress, like kaffir lime scented candles and orange fragranced body lotion from Provence. All of the furniture and jewelry is one of a kind stunning and very spendy, but so much fun to gaze upon.

PLUM

Zeitgeist gifts with a Nola accent

5430 Magazine Street (between Octavia and Jefferson)
+1 504 897 3388 / plumneworleans.com / **Open daily**

When I need an Elizabeth Ferguson Happily Ever After pillow for
an engagement gift, a pair of cockroach earrings for a Halloween
get-up or a Heather Elizabeth nightlight featuring the original Banksy
Umbrella Girl, I head to Plum, a beyond-quirky gift emporium.
Thanks to an owner with a sharp sense of zeitgeist leavened with
plenty of humor, this is the place for an off the wall gift or a present
for that special someone, even if it's yourself. Who knew I needed a
skull and crossbones festooned make up bag? Or that my bestie would
adore a silver Molly McNamara king cake baby flambeau charm? Better
yet, all that can't-live-without-it cache is on sale for not a lot of scratch.

SCRIPTURA

European style stationery boutique

5423 Magazine Street (between Octavia and Jefferson)
+1 504 897 1555 / scriptura.com / Closed Sunday

Growing up, I was taught the old fashioned art of writing proper thank you notes. There's something about a handwritten card as opposed to a text or e-mail that just seems more grateful somehow. Scriptura produces a high-quality line of stunning letterpress printed stationery and cards for all occasions, and does a bang up custom order business as well. They also sell every writing related thing imaginable, from silver wax seals to leather embossed journals. Although my previous attempts at swirly calligraphy were in vain, should I decide to try again, Scriptura is where I'll journey to for elaborate hand-blown glass fountain pens worthy of a lovesick Scarlett writing to her Rhett.

what to eat

Swoonworthy local bites

New Orleans is a Mecca for foodies; a hotbed of creative chefs marrying traditional Creole French fare with Gulf seafood and local ingredients in innovative ways. While everything is tasty, you can't leave town without eating the following goodies. Seriously. You just can't.

It doesn't matter that tourists flock to the original **Café du Monde** (see pg 38) for chicory-laced café au lait and beignets, deep fried fritters dusted with copious powdered sugar, three to an order. Locals love this 24/7 place because it's the best. We just don't wait in line on a Saturday morning.

Off the beaten track, the family run **Katie's** in Mid-City is a friendly neighborhood spot that serves a belly-busting cochon de lait po-boy, a two-hander stuffed with slow roasted tender pork and topped with horseradish-infused Creole coleslaw.

Situated in a back window of Erin Rose bar, an Irish pub just off of Bourbon Street, Chef Cam Boudreaux and his partner April Bellow deliver **Killer Po-Boys**, a revelatory take on the popular New Orleans sandwich. Forget fried oysters and roast beef debris, try international flavors like

KATIE'S

Moroccan-spiced lamb, five-spiced local meatloaf with hoisin glaze and local, wild-caught catfish piled with soy-cured green beans.

Proclaiming a favorite gumbo is fightin' talk around these parts – there are so many variations of the deeply simmered soup/stew, usually judged by the bronze of its roux and richness of ingredients. **The Gumbo Shop** does it right, with at least three variations always on the menu, including my own favorite, the seafood okra.

Although **Central Grocery** does deliver a good muffuletta, when I want a Dagwood of stacked Italian meats and cheeses garnished with chopped green olive salad, I go to Donald Link and Stephen Stryjewski's **Cochon Butcher**, a palace of piggy goodness that dishes a killer version stuffed with house-cured meats.

Save room for dessert at the handsomely redone **Brennan's** (see pg 53) on Royal. After an infamous cocktail-fueled Breakfast at Brennan's, a three-hour process powered by the likes of turtle soup and New Orleans classic Eggs Sardou, it's time for the floor show, tableside Bananas Foster, an iconic flambéed dessert invented in this very restaurant in the 1950s.

CENTRAL GROCERY
923 Decatur Street (between Saint Philip and Dumain)
+1 504 523 1620, centralgroceryneworleans.com
closed Monday

COCHON BUTCHER
930 Tchoupitoulas Street (at Andrew Higgins)
+1 504 588 7675, cochonbutcher.com, open daily

GUMBO SHOP
630 Saint Peter Street (between Chartres and Royal)
+1 504 525 1486, gumboshop.com, open daily

KATIE'S
3701 Iberville Street (at Telemachus), +1 504 488 6582
katiesinmidcity.com, open daily

KILLER PO-BOYS
811 Conti Street (between Bourbon and Dauphine)
+1 504 252 6745, killerpoboys, closed Tuesday

COCHON BUTCHER